Words

to Heal

the

Heart

Jonathon Lazear

A Fireside Book Published by Simon & Schuster

New York London Toronto Sydney Tokyo Singapore

Remembrance of Mother

F I R E S I D E

Rockefeller Center

1230 Avenue of the Americas

New York, New York 10020

Copyright © 1994 by Jonathon Lazear

FIRESIDE and colophon are registered trademarks of
Simon & Schuster Inc.

Designed by Bonni Leon-Berman

Manufactured in the United States of America

10 9 8 7 6 5 4 3 2 1

Library of Congress Cataloging-in-Publication Data

Lazear, Jonathon.

Remembrance of Mother : words to heal the heart / Jonathon Lazear.

   p. cm.

   "A Fireside Book."

   1. bereavement—Psychological aspects. 2. Mothers—Death—
Psychological aspects. 3. Mothers and sons. I. Title.

BF575.G7L39 1994

155.9'37'0852—dc20   94-1579

                                               CIP

ISBN: 0-671-88696-7

To

Virginia Cotton Lazear

1910–1992

Alice Jonas Broad

1911–1980

Acknowledgments

Love and gratitude to my mother, not yet gone a year, but who, since her death, has taught me a great deal. I never realized how much one can receive if one is open to it.

My gratitude and love to my "first" editor and wife, Wendy. She always has time to listen, and knows, too, when silence is as meaningful as speech.

To my father, my sister Conni, and my brother Chris, who took their own paths these past months. I'm not certain where your journeys took you, but I know you've all traveled far.

To my children, Ross and Michael, who, without knowing it, have been a comfort to me, and carry on some vestige of my mother through their acts and deeds.

To Tim Claussen, who was enormously thoughtful when my mother died. He contributed to the book, in more ways than one.

To my friend Anne Wilson Schaef, who continues to be the pioneer in healing. She, too, knows how to listen.

To my friends, who support me in many ways; Susie Moncur, my talented and thoughtful assistant; and Eric Vrooman and Dennis Cass, for their warmth and humor.

To Evelyn Friedberg and family.

And finally, to Sheila Curry, a great editor who brings wit and wisdom to her work; and my respect and friendship always to Marilyn Abraham.

Jonathon Lazear
Minneapolis
November, 1993

Clearances No. 3

When all the others were away at Mass
I was all hers as we peeled potatoes.
They broke the silence, let fall one by one
Like solder weeping off the soldering iron:
Cold comforts set between us, things to share
Gleaming in a bucket of clean water.
And again let fall. Little pleasant splashes
From each other's work world bring us to our
senses.

So while the parish priest at her bedside
Went hammer and tongs at the prayers for the dying
And some were responding and some crying
I remembered her head bent towards my
head,
Her breath in mine, our fluent dripping
Knives—
Never closer the whole rest of our lives.

—Seamus Heaney

Loss

$\mathcal{L}$oss. It is at once different for everyone, and yet the same. As Maya Angelou says, "We are human. Human beings are more alike than unalike."

But this first morning I wake, after my mother has died at a little past two A.M., I am numb. I have slept late; my wife has returned from taking the children to school, and so here we are, together, looking at one another. My first inclination is to call my father, to make certain he's "okay." I had said good-night to him at about four A.M., but now it is nearly ten, and I am afraid of how I will find him.

I call, and am relieved to hear his voice. He tells me he has begun calling those who were close to my mother. There are few left. She died just short of her eighty-second birthday, and, I am reminded many times, most of her contemporaries, friends, and family members of the same generation are gone. Those are people she had to mourn, to grieve over, to say good-bye to.

I feel the need, and I believe so many of us do, to take care of my father. They were together some sixty years. I begin the arduous task of submerging my grief, anger, guilt—my sense of loss.

I have begun my role as caretaker.

*T*here's a real cliché that is prevalent, and, I think, potentially damaging. It tells us that we should "get busy" after a loss. Go back to work; become immersed in the day-to-day routine.

Getting busy is denial in action. If you fill your days with appointments, obligations, meetings, and deadlines, you'll successfully bury your sorrow—but you'll later harvest more anguish than you can believe.

I've actually heard survivors say, "I just don't have time to think about it, and that's good."

The *best* thing to do is feel. You need to take that first step, and it's probably the most painful step you'll ever take. You have to face your mother's death; you have to admit your loss and remember what she meant to you, including your disappointments, your sorrows, your anger. Only after this step will you be able to take others.

*D*eath came very easily to her. She had lived such an innocent and loving life of service to others and held such a simple faith, that she had no fears at all and did not seem to mind very much."

—Sir Winston Churchill, on the death of his nanny

My friend Bob began confronting his loss over a long period of time. His mother's fight to conquer her cancer was so protracted that Bob felt his loss, little by little, over two and a half years.

The days his mother raged against her pain, her surgeries, and her chemotherapy never allowed Bob to begin the process of saying good-bye. While he wanted her to do battle with this disease, he also knew it could never be won.

His grief began before his mother died. He felt he lost her some months before her actual passing. So determined was she to win, she began to deny what was happening to her. This left Bob and his brother to either confront her with the reality of her terminal illness, or to join her in denial. Bob's grief began when he started to see that her self-delusion wouldn't save either of them.

a man never sees all that his mother has been to him until it's too late to let her know that he sees it."

—William Dean Howells

*I*t has been nearly a year since my mother's death. I want to become "unstuck," as some professional grief counselors put it; being "stuck" is the need to play the same memory tapes over and over that retain the same inner messages—

> If only I had . . .
> If we had just another . . .
> I hope she knew . . .
> Wouldn't she have loved . . .

ℳy mother nearly smothered me with love."

Joan is angry and frightened, and she doesn't know what to do about her mother's sudden death.

"She controlled me from birth until yesterday. Yes, I loved her, but I had no idea that she had such a hold on me. Now I feel almost betrayed, like she dropped me into the ocean and said, 'Swim.'

"I don't know where to begin with this grief business, because I guess I'm just too angry to face it yet. Why did she have to be on top of me all the time?

"We fought, but it always got resolved. Now she's really abandoned me, and I'm feeling really lost."

$\mathcal{P}$eople are like puzzles, and when somebody special dies, there's a feeling that those particular pieces will never be assembled again—that particular picture is gone."

—*The New Yorker*

$\mathcal{D}$eath is as casual—and often as unexpected—as birth. It is as difficult to define grief as joy. Each is finite. Each will fade."

—Jim Bishop

*T*hese repeated memories became enshrouded in a web of self-imposed isolation. This act of self-flagellation gets us nowhere—which sometimes is exactly where we want to be. But what of the rest of our lives? Would our mothers not have wanted us to carry on, to be happy?

$\mathcal{A}$mother understands what a child does not say."

—Jewish proverb

We just lost Mom, and after almost two years of taking care of her, I feel relieved and feel guilty for feeling relieved."

Those were the words of Nancy, our friend who, with the help of her brother, had taken turns looking after their Alzheimer's-afflicted mother. It wasn't just relief she was feeling. Nancy also was angry and hurt. After all the time and effort of taking care of her mother, at the expense of caring for her family and herself, her mother would never be able to thank her or realize how devoted Nancy had been. Their roles of caretaking had shifted. Nancy's guilt and anger and relief were intermixed with her feelings of loss.

$\mathcal{A}$t first, I want to talk about my mother—even the details, her last days, hours, minutes. I think this is because I'm supposed to be one of the "enlightened" ones regarding loss and mourning and grief and "processing" feelings. But now it is too hard. I see my father, my sister, brother, relatives, and friends. At the funeral I have successfully submerged my profound sadness. I no longer want to talk about her, reminisce, look at old photographs, even reenter my parents' apartment. It is too hard. And it really should be. I will talk about her and confront her death when I can.

$\mathcal{A}$t first, we just walked—together. As I look back, when she first joined me, I shifted from wandering to walking. At the time, I was barely conscious of her being at my side, and yet, I did know that someone had joined me. I was aware of a presence walking with me. Still, in the engulfing enormity of my pain, I could only respond inwardly with integrity, and those walks were my time not to have to care for others' grief. She did not seem to need response, so I gave none. We walked in silence. After a time, we walked in companionable silence. There was no need for anything to pass between us. We were alone, together."

—Anne Wilson Schaef, *The Grief Woman*

$\mathscr{M}$other died today, or maybe it was yesterday."

—Albert Camus, *The Stranger*

The finality of my mother's death really does not "sink in." Because there were periods of time when I did not see her, her absence from my day-to-day life does not seem abnormal.

When someone you love dies, and you're not expecting it, you don't lose her all at once; you lose her in pieces over a long time—the way the mail stops coming, and her scent fades from the pillows and even from the clothes in her closet and drawers. Gradually, you accumulate the parts of her that are gone. Just when the day comes—when there's a particular missing part that overwhelms you with the feeling that she's gone, forever—there comes another day, and another specifically missing part."

—John Irving, *A Prayer for Owen Meany*

$\mathcal{B}$y nature, I'm an emotional loner. For a variety of reasons, so many of us are the same with respect to showing our sadness as well as our happiness.

But something odd happened to me. At the funeral home, when relatives and friends came to visit, I was open with them, I allowed them in. I needed them, I needed to hear what they said about my mother, and somehow, and for some reason, for once, I did not turn away, but instead began to feel a connectedness with others in the room. I realized *all* of us were grieving, and we all *needed* one another.

$\mathcal{H}$ad Julie not been deceased, it was a funeral she would have loved.

"The minister, in his desperate struggle for an analogy of comfort, said to her three sons sitting rigid in the front row, 'Think of your mother as the spirit leaving the body. The shell is here, but the nut is gone.'

"The organist forgot the music and the only song she knew by heart was 'The Days of Wine and Roses.'

"And her middle son, Steve, flew in from school with only the shoes on his feet . . . a pair of red, white, and blue Adidas with stars that glowed in the dark, which he wore with a three-piece brown suit.

"It was hard to believe Julie was dead, at forty-eight, the victim of a 'kind' cancer that acts quickly and with accuracy."

—Erma Bombeck, *Motherhood: The Second Oldest Profession*

$\mathcal{T}$he hand that rocks the cradle is the hand that rules the world."

—William Ross Wallace

In some ways, we lose our way when our mothers pass on. We may have jobs, obligations, social functions that must be attended; but when our mothers are gone, suddenly we're rudderless.

Our world, when Mother dies, is upside down. Our emotional equilibrium is threatened, and most of us don't understand why we're adrift for so many reasons.

Mother was everywhere. We sought her assurances and acknowledgments in the most peripheral ways. We miss her for reasons we don't understand.

After all, we were barely able to see when hers was the hand that rocked our cradles. We do go on, though, and remembering her love is what keeps us going.

*I*n the days following my mother's death, I adopt the same erratic rasping cough she had the last few days of her life. To my ears, it is identical. I wonder how I could mimic the sound of it, how completely I had taken it on, as if I were somehow extending her life by imitating her. Later I learn that this phenomenon is not unusual. Often people who are very close with the deceased have "unexplained" components of the illness that befell their loved one. It's called sympathetic illness. I am surprised by this, but in an odd way, I'm comforted by it, too.

*B*lessed sister, holy mother, spirit of the fountain, spirit
of the garden,
Suffer us not to mock ourselves with falsehood
Teach us to care and not to care
Teach us to set still
Even among these rocks.
Our peace in his will
And even among these rocks
Sister, mother,
And spirit of the river, spirit of the sea.
Suffer me not to be separated
And let my cry come unto Thee."

—T. S. Eliot

$\mathcal{L}$osing mother has meant, among many things, that the remaining family, my father, my sister, and my brother, must now come together, if only figuratively. We now share an undeniable experience: we have lost a mother; my father, his wife.

We all feel the loss differently. She was a different person for each of us. Looking at us as honestly as I can, I see that she left behind three extremely different children. But now we share the commonality of grief; now we are forced to reflect on what we've lost and what the loss means to us.

I cannot dictate how my brother should feel, nor can I expect my sister's bereavement to echo mine. I do hope this inevitable tragedy brings us closer together.

*G*rant me the ability to be alone;
May it be my custom to go outdoors each day
among the trees and grasses,
among all growing things
and there may I be alone,
and enter into prayer
to talk with the one
that I belong to."

—Rabbi Nachman of Bratzlar

Grief

$\mathcal{A}$lthough I do not know why, and perhaps never will, one of my siblings had not been in touch with my mother at all for over two years before her death.

I don't know whether it was because of fear—seeing Mother deteriorate—or because of denial, but it hurt those of us who remained in contact with her.

Mother never got to say good-bye—nor did they even share a "last" conversation.

I believe that my family member who was aloof and unreachable during those years probably suffers silently, secretly, now.

*T*he death of our mother is a major change, one that brings about a profound change in our lives.

We do so well with denial, and death is one of the "events" in our lives that we're quick to turn from. If we know it's coming soon, we face the other way. If we are taken by surprise by an "untimely" death, then we can easily fall into denial coupled with anger.

*R*ight now that word 'joy' may choke you. . . . For anyone, newly grieving, to take even this first step is as difficult as learning to walk for the first time. You are, in fact, back at the beginning of learning to live again, to function, to participate in life. You are learning to live the second part of your life, so be patient with yourself."

—Eugenia Price, *Getting Through the Night*

$\mathcal{T}$he ultimate lesson all of us have to learn is unconditional love, which includes not only others but ourselves as well."

—Elisabeth Kübler-Ross

This vague other-worldly feeling must be similar to what is known as "going into shock" as a result of an accident. Days, even weeks after her death, I don't have the same "self-awareness" that I normally do. I feel "out of body," an onlooker; I feel like an observer, not a participant. Secretly, I know that this is another way of distancing myself from the reality of her death.

*E*ach person has his own safe place—running, painting, swimming, fishing, weaving, gardening. The activity itself is less important than the act of drawing on your own resources."

—Barbara Gordon

$\mathcal{I}$ do not think I have consciously decided to prolong my bereavement. In fact, I'm fairly aware of how I want to move through the stages of grief. But things remembered pull me back, causing depression and suffering. The holidays are upon us, her favorite time of year.

I know I must not dwell on this, but I also know that, to some extent, I must give in to it. Part of my process is to allow myself to *feel* the grief, not just talk about it.

Sorrows cannot all be explained away . . . in a life truly lived, grief and loss accumulate like possessions."

—Stephan Kanfer

hat restraint or limit should there be to grief for one so dear?"

—Horace

*Y*ou need to give yourself to grief. It does no good to deny it. It does no good to attempt to rationalize it, overthink it, intellectualize it.

You would not rise up from the pavement and go about your business after being hit head-on by a bus. The pretense of strength, willpower, or stoicism will protect you for a while but later, just when you think you're above and beyond it, grief will have its way. Then you will feel profoundly and suddenly alone. Not allowing the process to direct you in a natural healing way will create a festering and incapacitating isolation later.

$\mathcal{H}$e sows hurry and reaps indigestion."

—Robert Louis Stevenson

*I*f I feel detached—and I've created a distance with reality on purpose—I know it is because I do not want to acknowledge her absence. Still, in middle age, I want to feel the buffer, certainly imagined, but real to me, that she created for me. She was my protector, my comforter, my ally. I feel adrift when I begin to acknowledge her death. But I am still numb, and try to hide behind the numbness, and let this strange limbo take over, like a mist, like a fog.

I know well what I am fleeing from but not what I am in search of."

—Montaigne

$\mathcal{T}$his is hard. One of the hardest things I've ever had to do. I'm supposed to be well equipped to deal with emotional upheaval. I know how to cope.

But I find myself going inward, gradually creating a silent emotional habitat. Strength is a virtue, we've all been told. So be strong; remain stoically silent. Hide your bereavement and it will go away.

I know this is a damaging thing I'm doing. It causes a decaying of the healthy coping I've tried to adopt and practice. So each day now, I try to express my grief in outward ways. I read about loss, or I look at family photographs, or I go to sleep with pleasant memories of my mother, from earlier days, when we didn't think of losing one another.

$\mathcal{B}$eware the easy griefs that fool and fuel nothing."

—Gwendolyn Brooks

$\mathcal{H}$alf our mistakes in life arise from feeling where we ought to think, and thinking where we ought to feel."

—J. Churton Collins

I feel like I'm operating on two levels: One is the outward me—the one I project to those close to me. It's cordial and reserved. The second level is the dark harbor I have been left with—my point of view of the world is now totally skewed. I feel withdrawn, aloof, almost watching my own life from above. I believe this atmosphere of detachment comes from anger and denial. But now it is a vivid, memorable feeling.

"*I*s there no pity sitting in the clouds,
That sees into the bottom of my grief?"

—Shakespeare, *Romeo and Juliet*

*a*fter time has passed since her death, I don't really miss the attention or the pity that friends and business associates had been giving me. I feel like I want to withdraw from everybody. Even my immediate family offers me no comfort. I tell myself this is a singular experience. No one can possibly know the profound loss I feel. They cannot possibly remember those moments when I felt particularly close with my mother, when she defended me, took my part, sheltered me. But I will never forget those times.

*I*n deep sadness there is no sentimentality."

—William S. Burroughs

I must say, I feel more free, and curiously less pressured, to move on in an artificial way with my grief. For whatever reasons, I may *need* to be depressed rather than angry now. It is, after all, *my* process. I must travel this path at my own pace with my own stopovers and detours.

*P*eople in distress never think that you feel enough."

—Dr. Samuel Johnson

I understand that I need to stop shunning reality. I know that I must acknowledge my loss. I also know that my brother, sister, and father are all experiencing my mother's death differently than I am. I do not share the anger that resides and festers with one of them; I do not have the hard, nearly impenetrable exterior that another has. And I know for sure that my father's grief and sense of loss are different from my own. In the days that pass I understand one thing, and it is something that I come to by myself, for myself: the more I allow myself this grief, the more I can open up to what I'm told is the "process" of grief. When I am open to begin dealing with it, I will be better able to cope with it.

$\mathcal{T}$rue guilt is guilt at the obligations one owes to oneself to be oneself."

—R. D. Lang

$\mathcal{F}$or a while I tried to force my process into the exact molds of time and experience that certain grief specialists insisted were the order in which various stages of bereavement appear. I am told by a wise counselor that everyone who undergoes grief when they lose their mother experiences unique bereavement. "Yes," he said, "there are many similarities in the grieving process—denial, anger, remorse, et cetera, but everyone's process is different, because everyone's relationship with their mother is different."

ou never find yourself until you face the truth."

—Pearl Bailey

*P*eople who grieve always say, "Today I saw a friend and wanted to call my mother to tell her," or "I was aimlessly thinking about how and where we'd spend the holidays, and then remembered that Mother would never be with us again."

We cannot go back. And part of our early grief comes from this terrible sense of finality.

We will never be the same person again. Our family is unbalanced. There is a hole in our hearts, and it feels as though it may never heal.

𝒯his morning I wake up, and remember a dream I had about my mother. I recall it with such clarity, in such remarkable detail, that I am actually buoyant when I get out of bed.

*I*t is only then that I realize that I'm beginning to feel my mother's loss. My dream has been a very memorable conversation with her; we are laughing, reminiscing, hugging, and commiserating. It is a perfect dream of a person who is gone. We are totally in sync and happy. Oh, how I miss her, and God, am I really beginning to feel it.

$\mathcal{Y}$esterday I dared to struggle. Today I dare to win."

—Bernadette Devlin

$\mathcal{L}$ooking back," says my friend Steve, "those were dark days."

Steve's mother died about three years before my mother died, and he is, for my benefit, recounting his grief process.

"At first all of us were numb—really detached. But in the months that followed my sister and brother and I became closer. We really checked in with one another, and as our grief diminished, our relationship grew stronger.

"Sometimes I wonder if that was Mom's legacy. I'd like to think that it was."

My friend Melody, after the death of her son, wrote a book titled *A Reason to Live*. This wonderful little book is dedicated to the concept of moving on, allowing the process of healing to coincide with the new search for meaning coupled with the concept of choosing life over the darkness of the wasteland that grief can be. It is a simple but wise book. It teaches us that grief is a process, and growth is the product.

I do not think that I will ever reach a stage when I will say, 'This is what I believe. Finished.' What I believe is alive . . . and open to growth . . ."

—Madeleine L'Engle

$\mathcal{F}$or the first three months after Angela's mother died, she behaved like a virtual shut-in. Everybody tried to get her to come to dinner, see a movie, go shopping, to church, anything; just to get her back on track.

It worried a lot of us that she was so reticent to face her mother's death. We all felt she was wallowing in self-pity. But some weeks later, Angela started calling a number of us on the phone, making plans to see us, to visit her relatives, to get back to work full time.

Now our friend Angela is back on her feet, and is her old self. She seemed to pass through the fog of grief the only way she could.

It seems that not all of us grieve the same way. Whatever she was doing in the solitude of her apartment after her mother died was what she needed to do. Angela has reentered the world as the healthy, rational, wonderful person we knew. She just had to get through it *her* way.

Reflections

$\mathcal{T}$o nourish children and raise them against odds is in any time, any place, more valuable than to fix bolts in cars or design nuclear weapons."

—Marilyn French

$\mathcal{T}$he death of the mother is probably the most powerful thing that will ever happen to a child.

The trauma of the loss, whether anticipated or unexpected, creates suffering that may go "unhealed" throughout the rest of a person's life.

Children go through the same grief cycle that adults do. They first feel shock, perhaps coupled with denial, anger, withdrawal, and may not be able to resume any real semblance of normalcy in their lives.

Children, just as adults, need to be encouraged to grieve openly and without restriction. While most have an extraordinary capacity for adjustment, grieving is, nonetheless, a process that must be afforded the child who's lost his mother.

*C*l mother is she who can take the place of all others but whose place no one else can take."

—Cardinal Mermillod

$\mathcal{I}$t's been seven years since Mom died," Louise is telling us, "and I can still hear her voice. But the best thing is her laugh. Nobody had her laugh. It was infectious and loud, and just about everybody would crack up every time she got into a laughing jag."

Louise also tells us that not one family gathering goes by that at least one member of the family tries to duplicate her mother's famous laugh. "It sort of kept her alive all these years, and it certainly always made us remember her in the best ways—when all of us were happy. Maybe it sounds nuts to you, but it was a real gift to us."

*P*erhaps the greatest social service that can be rendered by anybody to the country and to mankind is to bring up a family. But here again, because there is nothing to sell, there is a very general disposition to regard a married woman's work as no work at all, and to take it as a matter of course that she should not be paid for it."

—George Bernard Shaw

*T*oday I spoke to a friend who recently lost her mother. She immediately said, "We so often didn't get along. I guess I took after my dad, or at least I was my dad's daughter. But it didn't matter that Mom and I had a stormy and distant relationship. The night she died I felt so close to her. Maybe because we had been at odds so long that that became our relationship, and like it or not, paradoxically, the abrupt end of that relationship left me bereft and feeling the most lonely I can remember being."

Each of us has his or her own deep ties to Mother. The problem for some of us is that we really don't understand that until it's too late.

$\mathcal{S}$omeday, perhaps change will occur when times are ready for it instead of always when it is too late. Someday change will be accepted as life itself."

—Shirley MacLaine

When Mom died," says our friend Suzanne, "I found listening to her sisters and brothers at the wake and after the funeral to be so comforting."

She goes on to say, "They had great stories about Mom, many of them I had never heard. It turns out that she was a real tease and a prankster when she was a kid. Later I found out that she had been given a scholarship to college—something I never knew.

"I don't know if it's true for everyone, but I do know that in my case, listening to family members was very helpful to me. It's the best advice I can give anyone who has lost their mom. Listen to what others have to say about her. Hear how others saw her, knew her, felt about her."

$\mathcal{D}$eath gives life its fullest reality."

—Anthony Della Villa, priest

$\mathcal{T}$he general outlook is not that the person has died, but that the person has lived."

—William Buchanon

*I*t was my friend Jeremy who said, "God, I don't think we laughed as hard or as long when Mom was alive—at least in the retelling of some of her antics—as we did when some of us kids got together."

He went on to say that his mother was such a staunch conservative that she had a very prescribed sense of humor, justice, and propriety.

"It was at least six years after her death that we gathered, and we're still telling stories about her."

No matter what your age—fifteen, thirty, fifty, seventy, it doesn't matter—death is always untimely.

*I*t is a myth to think death is just for the old. Death is there from the very beginning."

—Herman Feifel

*P*eople who lose their parents when young are permanently in love with them."

—Aharon Appelfeld

Shrinking away from death is something unhealthy and abnormal which robs the second half of life of its purpose."

—Carl Jung

$\mathcal{N}$o snowflake falls in an inappropriate place."

—Zen saying

*L*oss of control. The myth of control. Those of us who so feel the need for control are confronted in the most profound way with a sudden and irrevocable loss of control when our mother dies. How can this happen? Why couldn't we prevent it?

If we begin to think clearly, to understand that perhaps she needed to let go, that hanging on was too painful, too rigorous, or too demanding, then maybe we can understand that not only does our need for control have nothing to do with the realities of life or death, but that one's death is entirely out of our hands. This was my mother's death, not mine.

This can be a time for learning a great if painful lesson that may clear our lives of the debris of the myths we have created about control.

$\mathcal{T}$each me to live that I may dread
The grave as little as my bed."

—Thomas Ken

How selfhood begins with a walking away,
And love is proved in the letting go."

—C. Day Lewis

$\mathcal{T}$hay,' I said, 'my teacher, Katagiri Roshi, died four months ago. I studied with him for twelve years. I miss him very much.' I paused. My voice cracked. 'Where can I find my teacher now?'

" 'I knew Katagiri,' he said. 'He was a great man. For two summers, I invited him to Plum Village. He could not make it.' He nodded his head. 'He made it here this summer. You can find him here. In the trees. In the birds. He's here now.'

"I nodded. 'Thank you,' I said. I looked down. We went on to the next person. I took a sip of tea. I knew what he said was right, but I also knew I was not ready for it. I wanted the man, the human being. I wasn't ready to let go."

—Natalie Goldberg,
Long Quiet Highway: Waking Up in America

$\mathcal{T}$he Japanese Shinto religion is fascinating. The word *shinto* itself refers to "superior powers," natural or divine, that are held in the highest esteem by its followers.

In a home where Shinto is practiced, a shrine is erected, usually near the entrance to the home—it is a permanent place where, every day each member of the family stops to look upon it, and remember those elders in the family that have passed on.

It is a sacred rite of respect, and is, in part, a celebration of an individual's life from birth to old age.

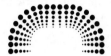

We all want to be happy, and we're all going to die . . . You might say those are the only two unchallengeable true facts that apply to every human being on this planet."

—William Boyd

*O*ur mother was the center of the family. She made all the arrangements for the holidays, family get-togethers, reunions, vacations, school functions—you name it, she was the planner and the instigator."

Pat and his sister Beth relate to me how, after their mother's death nearly two years ago, the family, even the extended family, started to fall apart.

"Since Mom was instrumental in getting all of us together, knew how to do it and when, she's been really missed. I guess you could say the guiding light of the family has been put out, and no one knows to whom the torch will be passed. She's been missed by everybody."

Often, a family who has a strong, warm, but dominant matriarch feels loss like the ripples across the water. She meant so much to so many, how do you ever fill the gap? She was not just a mother, but the hub of the family.

"We've created new traditions, and the division of labor has shifted now," said Pat. "We've accommodated our loss, but our family is just as strong. We're just missing one member, but we're getting along."

*I*t is only in the light of the inescapable fact of death that a person can adequately engage and enter upon the mysterious fact of life."

—John E. Hines, bishop, Episcopal Church

*A*nd did you get what you wanted from this life, even so?

I did.

And what did you want?

To call myself beloved, to feel myself beloved on the earth.

—Raymond Carver,

"A New Path to the Waterfall," from *Late Fragment*

Moving On

*R*ecollection can also be a wonderful healing activity. If one takes care of oneself while in bereavement, a good healthy moment of reflection can help move us along on our road to wholeness.

Keeping our memories alive by talking with others—brothers, sisters, friends, and relatives—is also a way of getting on with our lives without denying our loss. Clinging to memories of "the end" prolongs our pain, and gets us stuck in a rut.

Reaching out to others who have suffered your loss is often helpful—and remembering together is therapeutic.

I've been doing a lot of thinking
About growing older and moving on,
No one wants to think that they're getting on
And maybe going away
For a long, long stay.

"But just how long, who knows?
And how and where will my spirit go?
Will it soar like jazz on a saxophone,
or evaporate on a breeze?
Won't you tell me please

"That life is eternal
And love is immortal
And death is only a horizon
Life is eternal
As we move into the light
And a horizon is nothing
Save the limit of our sight."

—"Life Is Eternal"
Words by Carly Simon
Music by Carly Simon and Matthias Gohl

Marianne tells me when her mother died she was so angry and hurt, on top of her bereavement, because through-out her mother's illness—almost a year and a half—she was the child in the family to whom everything was left. She didn't mean the inheritance, but rather the hard work and dedication involved in overseeing her mother's health—getting her to doctor's appointments, to radiology, to chemotherapy, to physical therapy, and finally, arranging for hospice.

Marianne was also responsible for closing her mother's house, selling her furniture, and getting her into a nursing home.

But years later, Marianne is grateful that she was privileged to spend those last months with her mother, and she feels great comfort in knowing she truly experienced her love for her mother when her mother needed her most.

I hear her voice in his. I did before she died, but now it becomes ever more pronounced. My nine-year-old son exhibits speech patterns, eye movements, and other physical attributes that were passed along to him by my mother.

He has her eyes. I now see the lineage much more clearly than before. He takes after her in certain ways that make me stand in awe and amazement.

In this way, she is not totally gone. She appears and is heard in my house every day. I am so thankful for his traits, which were hers, too.

*H*appily may I walk.
May it be beautiful before me.
May it be beautiful behind me.
May it be beautiful below me.
May it be beautiful all around me.
In beauty it is finished."

—Navaho Night Chant

In beauty it is finished. The night. The end. This is a beautiful Native American prayer that speaks of beauty—and the end of the day.

I read this occasionally because it speaks to me of peace, of harmony with the earth, and with a reverence for the perfect cycles of life.

It renews my spirit, and I dedicate it to the spirit of my mother.

One of the mysteries that came to me in the months following my mother's passing was a series of extraordinarily vivid dreams that were remembered on awakening with the most minute voice, nuance, and detail intact. In these dreams my mother was always still alive; indeed, she seemed at her best—lively, funny, witty, laughing, and physically active.

I would wake up after one of these dreams always feeling that I had somehow had real contact with her; that we had communicated and were close once again. I was comforted by these nocturnal meetings. In fact, so intense were these dreams that I often try to recreate them.

Some things . . . arrive in their own mysterious hour, on their own terms and not yours, to be seized or relinquished forever."

—Gail Godwin

*F*or those of us who watched our mothers' health fail for years with chronic illness, or the downward spiral that is the final voyage of life, we think we are prepared for the ultimate: the day she no longer is alive.

I thought a thousand times over the last decade of my mother's life that I was ready for her death. Close calls, worsening medical conditions, occasionally inadequate medical care all brought her ever closer to death. I thought each crisis would be her last. Curiously, though, each time she was hospitalized I began to think she might pull through, because she had so many times before.

In the months that have passed, I have come to realize that she really did need to go. She did not feel invincible. Every rebound must have cost her dearly. A child doesn't always have that vantage point. I comfort myself with that, but I also believe it to be true.

When your heart is broken, your boats are burned: nothing matters any more. It is the end of happiness and the beginning of peace."

—George Bernard Shaw, *The Heartbreak House*

My father wants to make plans to move to a smaller apartment. I try to talk him out of it. "Why add to the trauma you're already suffering?"

I know instinctively that he needs to stay where he is. He needs to keep my mother's clothes in the closet, her purse on the dresser along with her jewelry box and perfumes.

In time, it will be the right time to remove her things. There might even be some joy in seeing other loved ones wearing her jewelry, a scarf or sweater. In some way her "things" help her to live on; they are tangible gifts that keep her memory alive.

*T*here is no need to run outside
For better seeing . . .
Rather abide
At the center of your being;
For the more you leave it, the
less you learn.
Search your heart and see . . .
The way to do is to be."

—Lao-Tzu

*I*f we have been close to our mothers, their death may force us to change the way we live. We know that we must make fundamental changes in our routines and our expectations, and we must not attempt to live our yesterdays again. As painful and as empty as we may feel, we must look to tomorrow to help us through today.

$\mathcal{N}$ow I'm aware that I alone am in the vast
openness
of the sea
And cause the sea to be the sea.

Just swim.
Just swim.
Go on with your story."

—Dainin Katagiri Roshi

There is no influence so powerful as that of the mother."
—Sarah Josepha Hale

I know that life must go on; the children need their father, as I do; my wife, although terribly saddened by my mother's death, nonetheless has moved beyond bereavement.

I am beginning to understand that cycle that I have read about. I now know that there is a season for all things.

Although I am now without my mother, I am clearer than ever about the time I have before me, and grateful for the time I had with her.

*D*o not stand at my grave and weep
I am not there. I do not sleep.

"I am a thousand winds that blow.
I am the diamond glint on snow.

"I am the sunlight on ripened grain.
I am the gentle autumn rain.

"When you wake in the morning hush
I am the swift, uplifting rush
of quiet birds in circling flight.
I am the soft starlight at night.

"Do not stand at my grave and weep.
I am not there. I do not sleep."

—Anonymous

*D*on't Grieve.

Anything you lose comes around in another form.

The child weaned from mother's milk

Now drinks wine and honey mixed.

God's joy moves from unmarked box to unmarked box,

from cell to cell.

As rainwater,

down into flowerbed

And roses, up from ground."

—from a poem by Rumi

Mother, you are gone. I think of you every day, nearly every hour, but you are gone. We will no longer see you at Christmas and Thanksgiving. You will no longer snuggle in your big blue chair with Ross.

We will not ever make one another laugh, or exchange information about friends and relatives. You'll no longer show pride in my accomplishments, or interest in the stories I tell about well-known writers and artists.

We won't share a meal; I won't introduce you to a new exotic recipe, show you a movie, or take you out to dinner.

You will not be able to give us your insights on family matters and members; our family history, before your time, is now mute. There is no one to convey our lineage, at least not the way you did.

You are gone, but I've chosen to move on, just as you'd have me do. I will try to be a better father and husband, not just for you, but, in part, because of you.

$\mathcal{N}$o one knew you quite like I did. And my father and siblings would say the same. I do think, though, that you and I spoke the same language, shared the same sensitivities; our humor was perfectly in sync.

No one can alter my memory of you and what you meant to me. I'll see you in so many places, hear your voice through memory, and keep our secrets to myself.

I miss you, yes, but it is time to look forward again, just as you'd want me to.

$\mathcal{D}$orothy Canfield Fisher once wrote, "A mother is not a person to lean on, but a person to make leaning unnecessary."

Although I miss my mother, I thank her for helping to make me independent of her. In her own ways, she modeled independence and self-reliance without showing indifference.

I try to remember that when I think of her, and when I think of my children, and how they will learn that lesson from their mother.

In Memory of Mother

I remember thee in this solemn hour, my dear mother. I remember the days when thou didst dwell on Earth, and thy tender love watched over me like a guardian angel. Thou hast gone from me, but the bond which unites our souls can never be severed; thine image lives within my heart. May the merciful Father reward thee for the faithfulness and kindness thou has ever shown me; may he lift up the light of his countenance upon thee, and grant thee eternal peace. Amen."

—Seamus Heaney

The following books were of great importance in my process of grief and the writing of this volume. I would recommend any of these wonderful works:

Bombeck, Erma. *Motherhood: The Second Oldest Profession*. New York: McGraw-Hill, 1983.

Coughlin, Ruth. *Grieving: A Love Story*. New York: Random House, 1993.

Goldberg, Natalie. *Long Quiet Highway*. New York: Bantam Books, 1993.

Kennedy, Alexandra. *Losing a Parent*. San Francisco: HarperCollins, 1991.

Kübler-Ross, Elisabeth. *Death: The Final Stage of Growth*. New York: Simon & Schuster/Touchstone, 1975.

Kushner, Harold S., Rabbi. *When Bad Things Happen to Good People*. New York: Avon Books, 1981.

LeShan, Eda. *Learning to Say Goodbye: When a Parent Dies*. New York: Avon Books, 1976.

Lightner, Candy, and Nancy Hathaway. *Giving Sorrow Words*. New York: Warner Books, 1990.

Myers, Edward. *When Parents Die*. New York: Viking Penguin, 1986.

Neeld, Elizabeth Harper, Ph.D. *Seven Choices*. New York: Dell Publishing, 1990.

O'Connor, Nancy, Ph.D. *Letting Go With Love*. New York: Bantam Books, 1989.

Roberts, Elizabeth, and Elias Amidon, editors. *Earth Prayers from Around the World*. New York: HarperCollins, 1991.

Tagliaterre, Lewis, and Gary L. Harbaugh, Ph.D. *Recovery from Loss*. Deerfield Beach, Florida: Health Communications, 1990.

Winokur, Jon. *Zen to Go*. New York: New American Library, 1989.